CONTENTS

Pianists on the recordings: [1]Laura Ward, [2]Brendan Fox

The price of this publication includes access to companion recorded accompaniments online,
for download or streaming, using the unique code found on the title page.
Visit www.halleonard.com/mylibrary and enter the access code.

ANIMAL CRACKERS

Christopher Morley

Richard Hageman

INTRODUCTION TO ART SONG

MEZZO-SOPRANO/ALTO

Songs in English for
Classical Voice Students

Compiled by Joan Frey Boytim

ISBN 978-1-4950-6465-4

To access companion recorded piano accompaniments online, visit:
www.halleonard.com/mylibrary

Enter Code
2105-0555-6278-3135

G. SCHIRMER, *Inc.*

DISTRIBUTED BY

HAL•LEONARD®
CORPORATION

7777 W. BLUEMOUND RD. P.O. BOX 13819 MILWAUKEE, WI 53213

www.musicsalesclassical.com
www.halleonard.com

PREFACE

Introduction to Art Song is intended for any beginning classical singer, teenager through adult. In most studios we have students who remain in traditional voice lessons for any number of years. As teachers, this gives us the time to determine the work ethic, the innate talent, and the personality of the student as we explore repertoire. In addition, we often accept beginning students who, for a number of reasons, will only be in our studios for a year or less. It seemed desirable to develop a book of previously successful, well-liked songs in English which are not particularly difficult, yet more mature than the *Easy Songs for Beginning Singers* series for use with these students.

A teacher browsing through the collections will find many familiar songs, but often in alternate keys from what has been previously published. Very often after recitals students will ask to sing a song they heard another singer perform from *The First Book of Solos* series, but it is not published in a suitable key. Some male voice examples: "When I Think Upon the Maidens," "Brother Will, Brother John," "Give a Man a Horse He Can Ride" and "Shenandoah." Female voice examples are "I Love All Graceful Things," "Danny Boy," "The Green Dog," and "Come to the Fair." In my own teaching some of my students will want to have their voice type appropriate volume of *Introduction to Art Song* for access to songs in comfortable keys.

Songs from American and British composers appear which are not included in previous collections. Of special interest are three, short, early songs by Samuel Barber only recently published: "Longing," "Thy Love" and "Music, When Soft Voices Die."

No sacred songs, Christmas songs or spirituals have been included, which makes the collections practical for use in beginning voice classes. The vocal ranges are moderate and the accompaniments are not extremely difficult. Each volume includes 15 to 20 songs.

This final set of four anthologies completes my various compilations of vocal repertoire books for beginning to intermediate singers, which began in 1991 with *The First Book of Solos*.

I want to thank my inspiring editor, Richard Walters, for believing in me, and offering his fine guidance, patience, friendship, and promoting the 60 published compilations, which I hope have made life easier for teachers all over the world. I also wish to thank Hal Leonard Corporation for giving me this amazing opportunity.

Joan Frey Boytim
compiler

The kit-chen's the co-si-est place that I know; The ket-tle is sing-ing, the stove is a-glow, And there in the twi-light, how jol-ly to see The co-coa and an-i-mals wait-ing for me.

Dad-dy and Moth-er dine lat-er in state, With Ma-ry to cook for them,

p

tre corde

36 Su - san to wait; But they don't have near - ly as much fun as I, Who

39 eat in the kit - chen with Nurse stand - ing by; And Dad - dy once said, he would

Lento

42 like to be me, hav - ing co - coa and an - i - mals once more for tea!

Tempo I

45

AUTUMN

Words by
Monica Hillier

Music by
C. Alison-Crompton

year. Clouds that rest _____ up -

on the hill - sides, Filled with

soft - est au - tumn rain,

Drift a - cross _____ the sad - dened

hea - vens Cry - ing, sigh - ing come a - gain: Come a - gain, oh sum - mer sun - shine, Come and kiss the dy - ing year.

for my mother
BLUEBIRD

Rudolph Schirmer

love me,— Leav - ing— me on - ly— a sigh.——

Don't you know Love will go Where the

blue - bird flies?——

COME TO THE FAIR

Helen Taylor

Easthope Martin

* The introduction may be commenced at the ⊕.

drums are all beat-ing, a - way let us go, ___ Heigh - ho!

come to the fair! There'll be rac-ing and chas-ing from morn-ing till night, ___ And

round-a - bouts turn-ing to left and to right, So it's come then,

maid-ens and men, To the fair in the pride of the morn - ing ___ So

121

hearts that are hap - py are lov - ing and kind, Heigh - ho!

127

come to the fair! __ If __ "Haste to the wed- ding" the fid-dles should play, __ I

133

war - rant you'll dance to the end of the day; __ Come then,

139

maid -ens and men To the fair in the pride of the morn - ing. __ The

THE GREEN CATHEDRAL

Gordon Johnstone

Carl Hahn

Slow and swaying

I know a green ca-the-dral, A

shad-ow'd for-est shrine, Where

* Or "ah"

to Miriam Witkin

THE GREEN DOG

Words and Music by
Herbert Kingsley

on it. _____ Shoes of leaf - green,

Hose of tea - green, Coat of ap - ple -green, Gloves _ of ___ bot -tle - green,

In fact, I nev - er would be seen ex - cept in

green If my dog were green.

LONGING
from *Two Poems of the Wind*

Fiona Macleod (William Sharp)

Samuel Barber

Allegro con grazioso

O __ would I were __ the cool __ wind __ that's blow - ing from __ the

sea, _____ Each lone - liest val - ley I would search till I should come to __

Tempo I

me— The grey si-lence, the grey waves,— the grey waste of the

sea._____ O— would I were— the cool— wind— that's

blow-ing from— the sea._____ Each lone-liest val-ley

softly *rit.* *opt.**

I would search till I___ should come to thee.

*The optional note appears in Barber's manuscript.

I LOVE ALL GRACEFUL THINGS

Kathleen Boland

Eric H. Thiman

INTO THE NIGHT

Words and Music by
Clara Edwards

find you there. I turn my gaze toward the morn-ing sun As from the east he comes thro' the dark and the dew; The flow-ers lift their heads- the night is gone- But where are you? The

count - less wea - ry steps__ I do not heed Tho' they be

o - ver land__ or bound - less sea; I care not where the road may

lead_____ If I but come a - gain at last to thee.

Si - lent - ly in - to the night I go, In - to the

star-ry right___ of heav-en-ly blue; What mat-ters where the road may

lead___ If I but come a-gain at last to you!___

Si - lent-ly, si - lent-ly

I come to you!___

A LITTLE CHINA FIGURE

Ethel Lindsay

Franco Leoni

Allegro con spirito

A lit - tle chi - na fig - ure On a lit - tle brack - et sat;— His

lit - tle feet— were al - ways crossed, He wore a lit - tle hat. And

ev - 'ry morn - ing, fair or foul, In shine or shad - ows dim,— A

84
die. And on the fol - low - ing morn - ing, when The shut - ters back she
f
88
ten.
thrust, She spoke his lit - tle ep - i - taph: "There's one thing less to
colla voce
p
92
f
dust. Ah! there's one thing less, one thing
gliss.
f
96
less to dust."
ff

MUSIC, WHEN SOFT VOICES DIE

Percy Bysshe Shelley

Samuel Barber

Rose leaves, when the rose is dead, Are heap'd for the be -

lov - ed's bed; And so thy thoughts when thou are gone,

Love it - self shall slumb - er on.

NO FLOWER THAT BLOWS

Thomas Linley

ORPHEUS WITH HIS LUTE

William Shakespeare
from *Henry VIII*

William Schuman

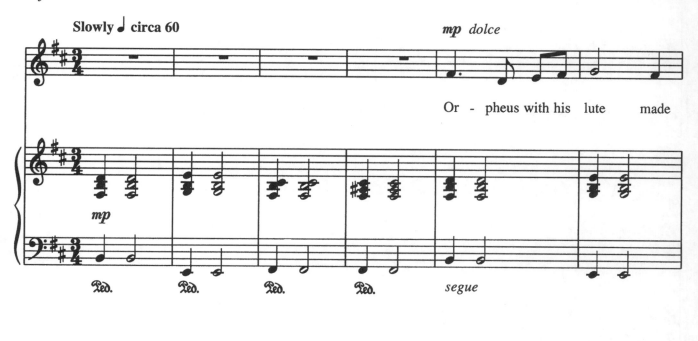

Or - pheus with his lute made

trees   And the moun-tain tops that freeze   Bow   them-selves when he did   sing:____

To his mu - sic   plants and flow'rs Ev - er sprung,   as sun and

THE POOL OF QUIETNESS

Grace Wallace

Thomas Vincent Cator

I am the dove that seeks the branch; But no mat - ter how far I fly, I shall re - turn to rest in your palm By - and - by, by - and - by.

A SECRET
from *Two Songs* (1903)

Roger Quilter

Quickly and brightly

My heart, my heart   No one may see,   It is lock'd a-

way   With a gold-en key   Till an - oth - er day,   till an-

oth - er day: _____   When my   love shall come,   As a

To G. S. Aunt Bess

THY LOVE

Elizabeth Barrett Browning

Samuel Barber

Barber indicated no tempo or dynamics in his manuscript.

WHEN DAISIES PIED

William Shakespeare
words from *Love's Labour Lost*

Thomas Arne

* optional melodic ornamentation for verse 2, by the editors
** appoggiatura possible

REWARD

Words and Music by
John Jacob Niles

bit - ter and long.___ When one fine day,___ one fine day___ you___ gath-ered me up,

And your arms were strong and your lips were warm And I saw a

world of which___ I had nev - er dreamed. It was a world a - new,___ a

bright, love - ly world a - new.___